G000075111

SPIRIT OF THE
LLANGOLLEN
RAILWAY

MIKE & KARL HEATH

First published in Great Britain in 2009

British Library Cataloguing-in-Publication Data
A CIP record for this title is available from the British Library

ISBN 978 1 906887 40 7

PiXZ Books
Halsgrove House, Ryelands Industrial Estate,
Bagley Road, Wellington, Somerset TA21 9PZ
Tel: 01823 653777
Fax: 01823 216796
email: sales@halsgrove.com

An imprint of Halstar Ltd, part of the Halsgrove group of companies
Information on all Halsgrove titles is available at: www.halsgrove.com

Printed and bound by Grafiche Flaminia, Italy

Introduction

Running, for approximately 8 miles, from Llangollen to the current western terminus at Carrog, this is the only operational standard gauge heritage line in North Wales.

For most of its length it follows the course of the River Dee affording excellent views of the dramatic Welsh countryside many of which are not available to travellers on the main A5 road which also follows the route higher up the valley side.

There are many pleasant walks through the splendid scenery starting and terminating at the railway's stations. Not surprisingly the line is the most popular tourist attraction in the area.

What follows is a stunning photographic journey along the length of the line capturing the spirit of the beautiful scenery, wonderfully restored country stations and variety of motive power that combine to provide a wonderful day out for both tourists and railway enthusiasts.

Occupying prime position in the town, Llangollen Station sits on the banks of the River Dee.

September 2006 and the railway's flagship locomotive ex-Great Western Railway Manor Class No. 7822 'Foxcote Manor' awaits departure from Llangollen with a freight train.

Left:
Between trains the crew of Pannier Tank No. 6430 enjoy the sun ahead of treating another train of passengers to the delights of the Dee Valley.

Right:
Having been given the right away 'Foxcote Manor' eases its train through the long platforms.

Left:
Sun, snow and freezing conditions offer a more dramatic scene with GWR 38xx No. 3802 producing a crisp white exhaust.

Right:
Another departure leaving Llangollen in the hands of ex-LMS Black 5 No. 44806. The previous views were from the bridge in the background.

Initially the railway climbs through a wooded section.

The River Dee flows past the foreground as 8F No. 48773, visiting from the Severn Valley Railway for the April 2006 Gala, forges its way towards Pentrefelin with a freight train.

In high summer 1991 Ivatt 2 No.46443, another visitor from the Severn Valley Railway, drifts towards Llangollen Station adding a bright interlude to a sea of green.

One time resident of the railway, U.S. Army-built S160 No. 5197,
nears journey's end with a return working from Carrog.

London and North Western Railway Coal Tank No. 1054 recaptures the days of the Edwardian branch as another freight train steams past in May 1997.

Just beyond Pentrefelin the railway makes its only crossing of the River Dee.

From Dee Bridge to the next station at Berwyn the railway climbs at a steady 1 in 80 grade. This gives impressive performances from engines and the sound echoes all around the valley.

TRAIN TO C

Berwyn Station encapsulates the traditional quiet Great Western Railway country station . . .

. . . albeit perched on a ledge high above the river below.

A Llangollen-bound freight drifts through the station.

The steep climb continues through the station causing engines to work hard all the way.
No. 3802 storms through with a non-stop working on March 4 2006.

For branch lines the Great Western developed autotrains where specially designed coaches with a driving cab at one end were coupled to a locomotive fitted with the necessary equipment. Here Pannier Tank No. 6430 is sandwiched between two such coaches as the ensemble restarts from Berwyn.

In summer the wooded valley is covered in dense green foliage which merely adds to the view of the valley and Chain Bridge.

However in winter all this greenery is gone and with a carpet of snow the valley becomes a winter wonderland. Saddletank 'Jessie' gives a towering display of steam whilst leaving the now extended station platform in March 2006.

The journey up
the line continues.

On several occasions the railway has operated an evening land cruise on the Thursday closest to Mid Summer Day. In 2002 this duty fell to No. 7817 'Garsington Manor' although all is not what it seems. In reality this is a disguised 'Foxcote Manor'.

The Horseshoe Falls, which feed the Llangollen Canal from the River Dee, sweep across the foreground with the railway clinging to the hillside above.

For the September 2007 Gala the railway hired in British Railways Standard Class 4 Tank No. 80136 which is seen here reflected in the tranquil River Dee just west of Berwyn.

Deeside is the midpoint of the railway where trains cross in the high season and during galas. In April 2007 the railway hosted the first 'Grange' Gala to raise funds to build a new member of the Grange class; one attraction of this gala was 3802 running in BR Black livery.

The railway's galas offer an intensive timetable demonstrated here by visitor 34081 '92 Squadron' which arrived shortly after No. 3802.

Above:
Autumn in the valley and a freight train rumbles through Deeside on its way to Llangollen.

Left:
The valley is subject to some unique lighting conditions and in this winter
scene shadows dance across the landscape as a train heads east.

The valley is once again gripped by winter with 'Jessie' powering through.

The trees that surround Deeside Halt create a dappled light over the railway's Black 5 No. 44806.

Also pausing at Deeside is the Autotrain. Unusually the coach is sandwiched between two locomotives!

Leaving Deeside behind the Black 5 continues up the line.

The 'USA' trundles through the Berwyn Hills at Garth-y-Dwr.

One of the 56xx class built for freight traffic in Welsh valleys by the
Great Western Railway, No. 5643 is on long term loan from the Furness Railway Trust.

The River Dee can be seen above the engine as Prairie Tank No. 5199
hauls a summer 2005 Llangollen-bound service away from Glyndyfrdwy . . .

. . . and onwards down the valley.

Above:
Framed by the signals National Railway Museum-owned
'City of Truro' arrives at the station during its 2005 visit.

Left:
Dwarfed by the scenery two winter walkers witness 'Jessie'
drifting towards the station on the final approach to Glyndyfrdwy.

Left:
Another view of the 2002 Midsummer land cruise, now standing under the footbridge.

Right:
Spring has sprung in this child's eye view of a Llangollen-bound train.

Left:
The embankments along the platform at Glyndyfrdwy always offer a riot of colour, enhanced here by the low evening sun.

Right:
In 2001 the Midsummer land cruise was in the hands of visiting ex-Great Western Railway Hall class No. 4936 'Kinlet Hall' which made a typically spirited departure from Glyndyfrdwy.

Once beyond Glyndyfrdwy the railway enters open country and runs parallel to the A5. Getting into its stride is No. 7822 'Foxcote Manor'.

Along this section engines get the opportunity to stretch their legs.

Left:
Inspiring vistas are open to all those who have chosen to travel by train.

Right:
Freight trains form a popular part of enthusiast weekends and here No. 5643 glides by with a rake of vans during September 2006.

Typifying the country branch line scene is the railway's 'Jinty' No. 47298 illuminated by the last of the day's sun. This engine now spends much of its time as a famous tank engine known all over the world as 'Thomas'.

Reputed to be the first locomotive to reach 100mph in 1904, 'City of Truro' coasts west along the valley on 9 June 2005.

Beneath Owain Glyndwr's Mount the railway is squeezed between the river and former castle motte. During the 2007 Grange Gala No. 78019, visiting from the Great Central Railway, re-enacts a 1950s' scene.

For the Grange Gala the railway hired in a 14xx tank engine which like its own pannier tank is able to operate with the autocoaches. Here this train scurries along the now wide floodplains to Carrog.

Left:
With Carrog just beyond the bend it was worth spending a few hours at this location as it wasn't long before we saw a returning train . . .

Right:
. . . or two!

Another view of the 2007 Grange Gala with visiting Great Western Railway heavy freight 2-8-0 tank No. 5224 on the final approach to Carrog Station. The valley's unique lighting is again in evidence.

The Grange Galas are organised to fund the construction of a new member of that class, similarly the railway held a Patriot Gala during 2008 to raise funds towards a new build of an LMS Patriot. For this gala two former LMS engines were hired in and are seen crossing at Carrog – they are 4F 44422 and Stanier Class 5 No. 42968 from the Churnet Valley and Severn Valley Railways respectively.

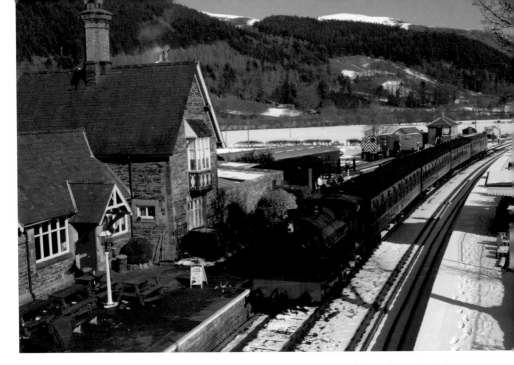

'Jessie' and Carrog station in a Christmas card scene viewed from the road bridge.

Characterising a busy gala is this shot of Pete Watermen's GW tank 5224 which has just come to a halt and already a train is steaming away into the distance.

The railway at Carrog runs across a wide flat valley.

The road down to the station offers splendid panoramic views of the railway.
Visiting 9F 'Black Prince' is seen heading a lengthy freight to Llangollen
leaving a crisp steam trail in the cold February air.

Above:
The railway is not exclusively steam and has recently started an annual DMU Gala. During the 2008 event visiting Railcar Unit 'Iris' stands at Carrog completing a 1960s' scene.

Left:
Looking west from the station bridge we see 'Half Cab' 41708 running round its train. Future trains will pass this point as the railway is currently extending towards Corwen.

Our journey has ended and we leave at dusk with the
last train of the day awaiting departure from Carrog.